THE APOSTOLIC ASSAULT TEAM MANUAL

A Guide to Strategic Global Spiritual Reformation of the Ekklesia

MARVIN HENRY

TABLE OF CONTENTS

DEDICATION

This manual is dedicated to my Lord and Savior Jesus Christ. It is also dedicated to the members of His Body who desire to work together as a unified team of believers to make maximum adversarial impact on the kingdom of darkness in the kingdoms of this world.

Additionally, I recognize and honor my wife Minna Henry who is also my best friend and co-laborer in the gospel ministry with me.

To my grandmother Mollie Day who was an apostle during an era when women were forbidden to preach. To my mother Barbara Green who taught me to reverence God as a very young child. To my spiritual coach and mentor apostle Melvin Thompson III who has fathered me in the gospel and prophesied life into my soul. And to all of the other men and women who have watered me along my life's spiritual journey.

KEY DEFINITIONS

Before we dive into this manual, please familiarize yourself with the terms listed below to provide a foundation for this teaching.

Apostolos – to be sent

Assault – to carry out a violent military attack or raid on (an enemy position).

Reformation – to return something to its original form, to amend or improve by removal of faults or abuses.

Ekklesia – the called out ones, the church

INTRODUCTION

It is necessary to understand the importance of this manual and the purpose of the body of Christ. The spiritual condition of the world demonstrates that the conscience of society is seared. In fact, society has been deceived so much, they call what is evil good and good evil. They put darkness for light and light for darkness. However, as God's children, we have a mandate from our Father. That mandate requires us to use the power, authority, and apostolic grace each one of us possesses as sons of God to overthrow the kingdom of darkness and usher in the kingdom of heaven.

WHO: This Apostolic Assault Team Training Manual is dedicated to you and every single member of the body of Christ globally and generationally regardless of your age, sex, creed, color or denominational belief.

WHAT: This Apostolic Assault Team Training Manual will show you scripturally how the apostolic grace of God desires to move through you and every single member of the body of Christ to recruit, train, develop, and implement victorious Apostolic Assault Teams in your family, churches, cities, regions, territories, and nations.

WHEN: The time to implement this Apostolic Assault Team training is now and continually.

WHERE: The Apostolic Assault Team Training Manual is to be implemented individually, corporately, and globally starting with you, your family, church(es), networks, and your ministry groups/tribes, etc.

WHY: Spiritual war is raging in our families, cities, regions, territories, and our nations. We must unite "globally" to fight and be victorious. It is not acceptable to sit idly by as the world perishes in unbelief because of the deception of the Enemy.

HOW: Apostolic Assault Teams are dispatched by the new commandment of Jesus Christ, filled and empowered with/by the Holy Spirit where all members pool their spiritual gifts together. They do so honorably among one another and flow in unity in the Spirit as one Man of War against the kingdom of darkness.

SHIFT THE MINDSET

We must change the way we are currently doing church and being the church. The way the church has evolved does not encompass what Jesus Christ had in mind when He died on the cross, rose from the dead, ascended into heaven, and sent the Holy Spirit to fill us with power to go into all the world and make disciples. Many of us have misunderstood the Great Commission and because of our misunderstanding, we have limited or zero knowledge about how to take the Ekklesia from the synagogue to society.

> And Jesus came and spake unto them, saying, All power is given unto me in heaven and in earth. Go ye therefore, and teach all nations, baptizing them in the name of the Father, and of the Son, and of the

Holy Ghost: Teaching them to observe all things whatsoever I have commanded you: and, lo, I am with you always, even unto the end of the world. Amen (Matthew 28:18-20, KJV).

The mindsets of the spiritual leaders in this nation must shift if we are going to bring our nation and this world back to God. This begins with understanding the Great Commission. When we read the commission that Jesus gave us, it becomes evident that the mindsets of many present-day churches are far from what Jesus instructed. It would appear that much of the body of Christ believes we are only responsible for those who come through the doors of our buildings, and maybe our surrounding communities. We minister to those few people and think that is all we are accountable for. This is a very limited and myopic view of the responsibility of the body of Christ. Jesus said <u>all</u> power is given in heaven and in earth. If we are the adopted sons of God, and we have the same authority, it makes sense why Jesus tells us to go, teach <u>all</u> nations, and baptize them. We limit God and the power of His Word by only focusing on what is within the four walls of a church building.

Spiritual leader, as Matthew 28:18-20 is amplified by the Holy Spirit, you will understand that the Ekklesia is a team. The Ekklesia is just one ginormous Apostolic Assault Team. As indicated in the definition, "Ekklesia" is the body of Christ. Many times, we reference "the church" as our local assembly. However, Ekklesia can be employed to reference the body of Christ over a region and even worldwide. We limit ourselves and our power when our focus is only on the local assembly. There is power in unity, and we are a much greater force as a united group of believers than we are as individuals or even single churches.

Spiritual Leader, as you continue to read, your mindset will shift. Then, Christ will use you to change the mindset of His Ekklesia, which He has given you oversight of. We are under an apostolic mandate to take governmental authority of our circles to bring revelation and truth of the Great Commission and our role in the kingdom. Ask Holy Spirit to open your heart and your mind to the revelation of a greater mandate and grace as we continue reading this manual.

Let's break down Matthew 28:18-20 to understand in a greater way the commission to the body of Christ. Jesus reminds His Apostolic Assault Team of their power in His name:

> Then Jesus came to them [The Ekklesia/His Team of disciples] and said, "ALL AUTHORITY in heaven and on earth has been given to ME" (See Matthew 28:18).

His disciples work together in honor and submission to Christ, as well as to one another as a unified company of believers. As His team of disciples, we have been given tremendous authority because of our identity in Christ.

According to Ephesians 1:23 and Ephesians 2:6, we have all authority.

> He put all things under His feet and gave Him (Jesus) to be head over all things to the <u>church, which is His body,</u> the fullness of Him who fills all in all (Ephesians 1:23).

He raised us up together and made us sit together in heavenly places in Christ Jesus, that in the ages to come He might show the exceeding riches of His grace in His kindness toward us in Christ Jesus (Ephesians 2:6).

God set forth His son born of a woman to redeem us that we might receive the <u>adoption</u> as sons. Because we are <u>sons</u> God sent the spirit of His son to our hearts. We are no longer slaves (to the law – works) but a Son and heir to God (Galatians 4:4-7).

Because we are sons of God (male and female), we are seated in heavenly places to rule and reign with Christ. With Christ as our foundation and chief cornerstone, we have authority and dominion over every demon, principality, and all rulers of darkness that have attempted to prevent us from launching an assault against the kingdom of darkness

Jesus tells His Apostolic Assault Team where to conduct apostolic assaults. Then He tells them what to do as they conduct the assaults.

Therefore, [Ekklesia - (Team of Disciples) go [assault all areas of the kingdom of darkness] and make disciples of all nations, baptizing them in the name of the Father and of the Son and of the Holy Spirit (Matthew 28:19)

The kingdom of darkness must be assaulted [overtaken] with the visible, tangible, manifested power of God. This can be accomplished by exposing the lost to the love and the presence of God everywhere that we find them. As the lost are exposed to the glory and presence of God, they will desire to draw closer and know Him.

And teaching them to obey everything I have commanded you (Matthew 28:20a NIV).

We know personally that the more we grow to love Jesus, the more we desire to please Him in every area of our lives. Therefore, we are instructed to teach obedience to the commands of Jesus Christ.

And surely I am with you always, to the very end of the age (Matthew 28:20b NIV).

Jesus reminds us that we have nothing to fear as He is right there in us conducting His assault through us. We have nothing to fear because He has given us the victory already. As we execute our assignment of apostolic assault, He guides and protects us.

The only way to take the Ekklesia from the synagogues to society is through the apostolic assault as a team. God never intended for His church to remain within the four walls of any building, isolated from the lost and wounded. He gave us clear commands, weapons, and strategies to release mass destruction on the kingdom of darkness, to set the captives free, heal the broken-hearted, and restore the lost. Just as in the Parable of the Great Supper in Luke 14:23, we have been commissioned to, "Go [there's that word again!] out into the highways and hedges, and compel them to come in, that my house may be filled."

Additional information on the strategies, schemes, and maneuvers in conducting apostolic assaults in your territory will be revealed later as we progress in our journey through this Apostolic Assault Team Training Manual.

Notes

Notes

CHAPTER ONE

GOD IS THE GOD OF WAR AND STRATEGIC ASSAULT

Did Somebody Say War?

That's right—war! Here is why you need to understand the importance of that word:

Massive, global, spiritual war is raging in our families, cities, regions, territories, and nations. We must unite to get into the fight and be victorious. We are at war spiritually! I repeat – the Ekklesia is at war against the kingdom of darkness globally, so please, pay close attention.

When any entity in the natural realm goes to war, it goes as a unified entity. It goes to war as one human individual. It goes to war as one team of human individuals. It goes to war as one unified family, nation, country or region.

As it is in the natural realm, so is it in the spiritual realm.

God is a God of War

The Lord is a MAN of War; the Lord is His name (Exodus 15:3, AMPC). #manofwar

The Lord will go forth like a MIGHTY MAN, He will rouse up His zealous indignation and vengeance like a WARRIOR; He will cry, yes, He will shout aloud, He will do mightily AGAINST His enemies (Isaiah 42:13, AMPC). #mightyunifiedMAN

Look, the sovereign LORD comes as a victorious WARRIOR; His MILITARY POWER establishes His rule. Look, His reward is with him; His prize goes before HIM (Isaiah 40:10, NET Bible). #HisUnifiedMilitaryPower

God's angels are angels of war as God is the God of the angel armies

Samuel said to Saul, "God sent me to anoint you king over his people, Israel. Now, listen again to what God says. This is the God-of-the-Angel-Armies speaking:" [LORD of Hosts] (1 Samuel 15:12, MSG). #AngelsofWar

God's people are people of war. David was a man of war. Elijah was a man of war. Sampson was a man of war. Samuel was a man of war, and we are people of war as well.

For in Him, we live, and move, and have our being (Acts 17:28).

Proclaim this among the nations: "Prepare for war! Wake up the mighty men, Let all the men of war draw near, Let them come up (Joel 3:9, NKJV).

For the weapons of our WARFARE are not physical [weapons of flesh and blood], but they are mighty before God for the overthrow and destruction of strongholds, [in as much as we] refute arguments and theories and reasonings and every proud and lofty thing that sets itself up against the [true] knowledge of God; and we lead every thought and purpose away captive into the obedience of CHRIST (the Messiah, the Anointed One (2 Corinthians 10:4-5).

Unity is the key when we advance to overtake the kingdom of darkness.

Every kingdom divided against itself is brought to desolation, and every city or house divided against itself will not stand (Matthew 12:22).

For how can two walk together except they be agreed? (Amos 3:3).

Once the body of Christ comes together as one body with different members and focus our agenda on eradicating the kingdom of darkness, there will be no hope for the Enemy to survive! Let us come together and gain a perfect understanding of the Great Commission and the strategy for our region. Let us inflict a massive assault on the kingdom of darkness to release every captive and destroy every yoke of bondage to bring the kingdom of heaven to earth.

God Is Our Commander

I AM the Commander-in-Chief of the LORD's army," He replied. Joshua fell to the ground before him and worshiped him and said, "Give me your commands (Joshua 5:14, TLB).

THE EKKLESIA IS TO CONDUCT SPIRITUAL WAR AGAINST THE KINGDOM OF DARKNESS GLOBALLY AS ONE UNIFIED TEAM/ARMY

Let's take a look at how God our commander lays out His strategic militaristic strategies in one of the conquests of Joshua against Ai. Then, let's see how that is applicable to us today in our families, cities, regions, territories, and nations as God commands us to assault all territories through His great Apostolic Assault Commission:

> Then the Lord said to Joshua, "Don't be afraid or discouraged; take the ENTIRE ARMY and go [Apostolic Assault] to Ai, for it is now (yours to conquer). I have given the (king of Ai) and (all of his people) to you. [2] You shall (do to them as you did to Jericho and her king), but this time you may (keep the loot and the cattle for yourselves). Set an AMBUSH behind the city (Joshua 8:1-29, TLB).

Here, in this text, Ai was a very real place, but spiritually, Ai represents the kingdom of darkness, which is located within the sea of humanity or within the kingdoms of this world.

God speaks to us today just as He did to Joshua back then. Don't be afraid or dismayed. Take the entire army. Take the entire Ekklesia and go on an apostolic assault. Every person in the Ekklesia is necessary for the plan to be executed without any vulnerability or weakness. With the Lord as our commander and protector, we have no reason to fear the Enemy or the outcome of our assault. When we obey God the commander's instructions, we are guaranteed victory.

God encourages us. His divine impartation causes the resilient warrior spirit to rise up within us. Through our confidence in our position in Christ and revelation of the power that we possess, it is our responsibility to mobilize on the earth to regain all of the territories that we have allowed the Enemy to possess.

God tells us to work together in love and unity to conquer demonic territories [His divine strategy - AMBUSH]. For the plan to work, not one soldier could be out of place; otherwise, it would have tipped off the people of Ai that there were more soldiers than they initially saw. Love and unity require honor and respect. There is no competition when we honor the gifts of each other and the positions God has appointed in the body Of Christ

God gives us the neck of the king of the kingdom of darkness.

> Then the Lord said to Joshua, "Point your spear toward Ai, for I will give you the city" (Joshua 8:18).

Joshua did as he was commanded. We must remember that we are not fighting *for* victory. Because of Christ's work on the cross, we fight from the position of victory. As He gives us the strategy (point your spear toward Ai) and we obey, He will also give us the victory over the kingdom of darkness in our regions.

God commands us to utterly destroy the works of the kingdom of darkness.

> So the entire population of Ai, twelve thousand in all, was wiped out that day (Joshua 8:25).

Surrendering in complete obedience to God our commander is essential to getting the victory.

God commands us to keep the loot and cattle [the ideas, finances, and witty inventions] of the kingdom of darkness for ourselves.

Only the cattle and the loot were not destroyed, for the armies of Israel kept these for themselves. (The Lord had told Joshua they could.) (Joshua 8:27).

When we are obedient and active in our purpose, we are rewarded by the One who promises us victory. As we execute the apostolic assault on the kingdom of darkness by keeping God's commands, He gives us access to the wealth and riches the Enemy had in his control.

Pay attention to the weapon that gives the Ekklesia its strength: unity. Lone-ranger Christianity is not and has never been ordained by God.

Look, the sovereign LORD comes as a victorious WARRIOR; His military power establishes his rule (Isaiah 40:10, NET).

Notes

Notes

CHAPTER TWO

THE MISSION OF THE APOSTOLIC ASSAULT TEAM

The mission of an Apostolic Assault Team is to locate, close, and destroy the kingdom of darkness by the power of God through the use of divine strategies and maneuvers. The Apostolic Assault Team repels the kingdom of darkness' assault by the manifested visible power and demonstration of the Word of God and the love of God. It does so by engaging the kingdom of darkness in people, cities, regions, and territories in order to completely eradicate the deception that has overtaken the earth.

The Meaning of Assault

Webster's Revised Unabridged Dictionary

1. (*n.*) A violent onset or attack with physical means, as blows, weapons, etc.; an onslaught; the rush or charge of an attacking force; onset; as, to make assault upon a man, a house, or a town.

2. (*n.*) A violent onset or attack with moral weapons, as words, arguments, appeals, and the like; as, to make an assault on the prerogatives of a prince, or on the constitution of a government.

3. (*n.*) An apparently violent attempt, or willful offer with force or violence, to do hurt to another; an attempt or offer to beat another, accompanied by a degree of violence, but without touching his person, as by lifting the fist, or a cane, in a threatening manner, or by striking at him, and missing him. If the blow aimed takes effect, it is a battery.

4. (*n.*) To make an assault upon, as by a sudden rush of armed men; to attack with unlawful or insulting physical violence or menaces.

5. (*n.*) To attack with moral means, or with a view of producing moral effects; to attack by words, arguments, or unfriendly measures; to assail; as, to assault a reputation or an administration.

Jesus Christ Conducted Apostolic Assaults

Jesus Christ conducted apostolic assaults on the kingdom of darkness in heaven as He kicked Lucifer's butt out of heaven.

> And he said unto them, I beheld Satan as lightning fall from heaven (Luke 10:18).

Jesus Christ conducted apostolic assaults on the kingdom of darkness on the earth in the garden of Eden.

> And the Lord God said unto the serpent, Because thou hast done this, thou art cursed above all cattle, and above every beast of the field; upon thy belly shalt thou go, and dust shalt thou eat all the days of thy life (Genesis 3:14).

Christ conducted apostolic assaults underneath the earth as He descended and defeated death, hell, and the grave.

> For Christ also suffered[a] once for sins, the righteous for the unrighteous, that he might bring us to God, being put to death in the flesh but made alive in the spirit, in which he went and proclaimed to the spirits in prison, because they formerly did not obey, when God's patience waited in the days of Noah, while the ark was being prepared, in which a few, that is, eight persons, were brought safely through water (1 Peter 3:18-20).

> Jesus Christ is the same yesterday, today, and forever (Hebrews 13:8).

Jesus is still conducting apostolic assaults. He has already secured victory for the kingdom, and He will not rest until His kingdom is manifest and the kingdom of darkness is destroyed.

Jesus Christ executes apostolic assaults through His remnant of believers who can submit to and honor one another, so they can effectively work together as a team.

> For by the grace given me I say to every one of you: Do not think of yourself more highly than you ought, but rather think of yourself with sober judgment, in accordance with the faith God has distributed to each of you. For just as each of us has one body with many members, and these members do not all have the same function, so in Christ we, though many, form one body, and each member belongs to all the others. We have different gifts, according to the grace given to each of

us. If your gift is prophesying, then prophesy in accordance with your[a] faith; [7] if it is serving, then serve; if it is teaching, then teach; [8] if it is to encourage, then give encouragement; if it is giving, then give generously; if it is to lead,[b] do it diligently; if it is to show mercy, do it cheerfully (Romans 12:3-8).

Jesus Christ commissioned us to conduct apostolic assaults on the earth.

[Apostolic assault] Go into all of the world and make disciples (Matthew 28:18-20).

As stated earlier, God never intended for any of His people to be lone rangers. There is a blueprint for the operation in Scripture that we can duplicate.

God accomplishes His will on the earth through team ministry. God the Father, God the Son, and God the Holy Spirit do everything in unity with each other. The entire body of Christ is an Apostolic Assault Team, so we must all honor one another, submit ourselves and our spiritual gifts to one another, and work together in unity as well.

These five-fold ministry offices are to work together as a team to conduct global apostolic assaults in company with all of the other spiritual gifts in the body of Christ. 1 Corinthians Chapter 12 clearly instructs us that all members of the body of Christ are needed to conduct an apostolic assault. It describes the structure of the army to mobilize into formation for assault. There will be no schisms or divisions. Rather, each gift and office will honor the other as an integral member of the team to assault the kingdom of darkness. How can a city be taken unless it is assaulted?

God wants to use the five-fold offices in unison with one another and with all the other members of the body of Christ to assault the kingdom of darkness as one man or as one unified army.

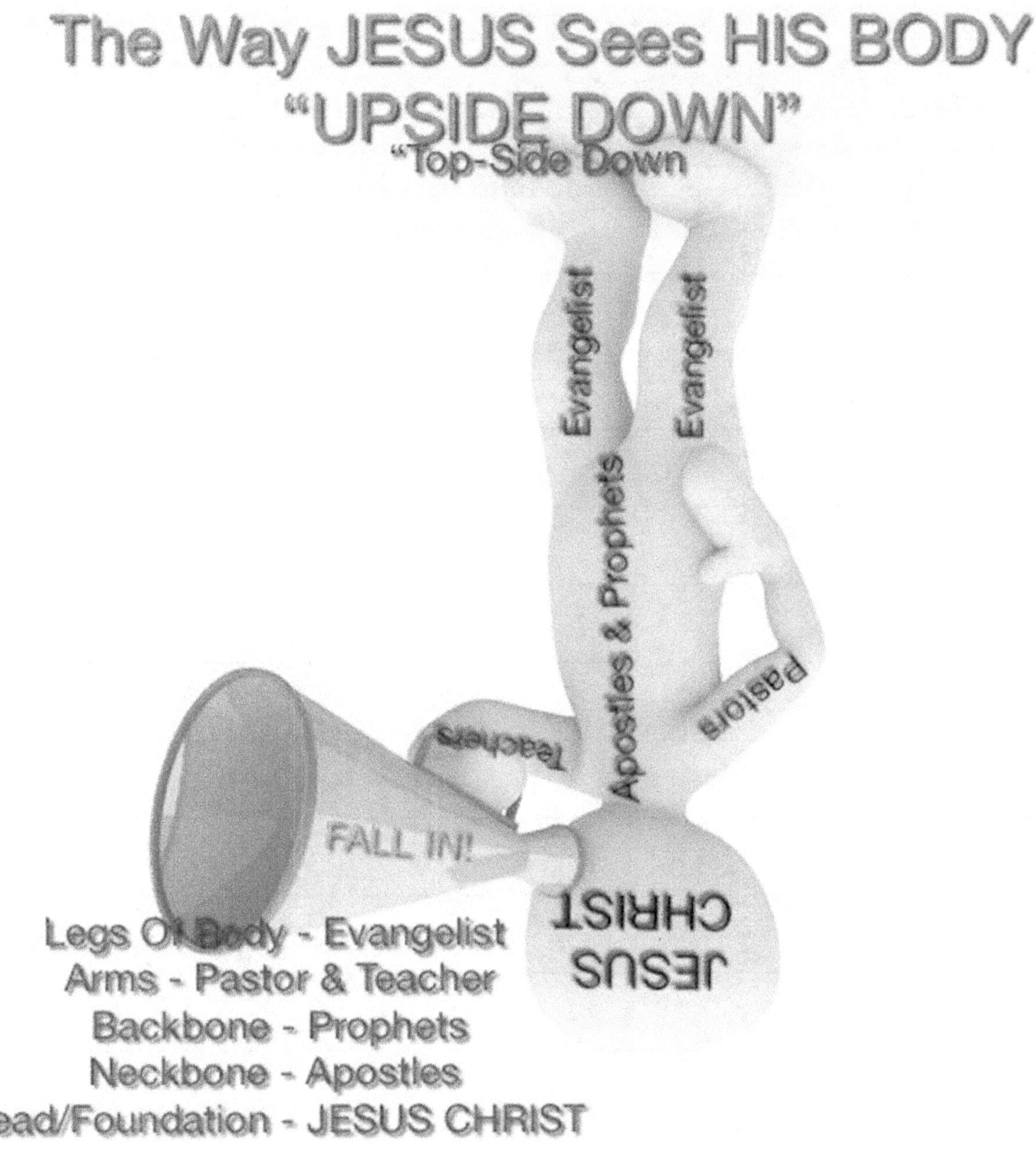

Notes

Notes

CHAPTER THREE

TOP-SIDE DOWN

In every army, there is a rank structure in God's army as listed below:

Here are some of the parts God has appointed for the church: first are apostles, second are prophets, third are teachers, then those who do miracles, those who have the gift of healing, those who can help others, those who have the gift of leadership, those who speak in unknown languages (1 Corinthians 12:28, NLT).

This clearly shows that the offices and the gifts are all a part of the same body and are intended to work together.

Jesus Christ Is the Head of the Body of Christ

He is the Head of the body made up of his people—that is, his Church—which he began; and he is the Leader of all those who arise from the dead, [a] so that he is first in everything (Colossians 1:18, TLB).

Apostles are the Neck & Prophets are the Backbone of the Body

Apostles and prophets are called the foundation of the church (body) in Ephesians 2:20: "And are built upon the foundation of the apostles and prophets, Jesus Christ himself being the chief corner stone." Without the foundation, a structure is unstable and easily collapses. If we also consider the backbone in the body, we understand that it is essential for the stability and healthy function of the body. For if the back or neck is weak or ailing, the body cannot stand for long. The function and range of motion of the arms and legs become limited when the back or neck is out of alignment or injured.

Pastors and Teachers Are the Arms of the Body

Arms provide a person the ability to perform basic functions and tasks necessary for the body to be healthy such as feeding, cleaning, and protecting itself from danger. Pastors and teachers can be seen as the arms of the body of Christ because they equip it by feeding the Word of God to protect, correct, cleanse, and comfort it. Just as in the natural, if a person's legs are injured for some reason, the arms are able to assist the body to mobilize; for instance, a baby pulling itself across the floor before its legs are able to support the body to crawl or by propelling a wheelchair forward. This mode of movement is not ideal, and a person in this condition would not be allowed to serve in the military, but it is adequate for necessary movement. The same principle exists in the spiritual realm. Without all parts of the body of Christ functioning at its full capacity, it is hindered from carrying out the operation effectively.

Evangelists Are the Legs of the Body

Just as the legs enable the body to move and become active to walk or run, evangelists mobilize the body of Christ to find and locate the lost. The heart

God gives the evangelist will mobilize a church to move out of the pews. Evangelists are integral in the organization of the army to deploy its apostolic assault beyond the four walls of the church building into the community, city, region, and world. The arms can enable the body to move when the legs are impaired or not strong enough to move the body independently. However, the legs that are fully functional are evidence of a healthy and complete body that is available for service.

All other members (spiritual gifts) are the remaining organs and parts of the body.

For example, the gift of discernment may be considered the eyes of the body of Christ. Without discernment, it will be more difficult to locate the lost and wounded to rescue and heal them. The gift of healing could be considered the heart of the body of Christ. For if healing does not take place in the body of Christ, life ceases to exist. Spiritually speaking, an unhealed or wounded person will hinder and diminish the vitality of a ministry, just as a damaged heart affects the energy and function of the body. The gift of helps and administration might be considered the hands and fingers of the body of Christ. For they enable the arms to attend to the fine details of a function or task.

Take some time to consider all of the specific gifts that exist in your body of believers and identify how they enhance the various functions of your ministry. When we discover how a gift highlights and enhances a specific area, we are better able to draw on the grace and anointing of that person's gift and add value to the Ekklesia as a whole.

FROM DEFENSE TO OFFENSE

All armies are structured to be confrontational, and the body of Christ is structured to be and must be confrontational as well. We must shift our mindsets from defending the attacks of the Enemy to an offensive strategy that infiltrates the camp of the Enemy to overtake and destroy the works of the kingdom of darkness, as well as rescue the oppressed and lost. We can no longer passively pray and wait for the unbeliever to walk through the doors of our churches, but we must actively and aggressively pursue them so they can be released from bondage.

The Kingdom of God suffers violence and the violent take it by force (Matthew 11:12).

God never intended for the church to be non-confrontational. "Go" in Matthew 28:18-20 means to confront, to assault, to be aggressive, to be hostile towards. God and even the children of this world know that the best defense is a good offense.

And He said to them, "Go [Apostolic Assault] into all the world and preach the gospel to all creation (Mark 16:15).

And as you go [Apostolic Assault], preach, saying, 'The kingdom of heaven is at hand' (Matthew 10:7).

And He sent them [His Body] out to [Apostolic Assault] proclaim the kingdom of God and to perform healing (Luke 9:2).

But He said to him, "Allow the dead to bury their own dead; but as for you, go [Apostolic Assault] and proclaim everywhere the kingdom of God" (Luke 9:60).

Go [Apostolic Assault], stand and speak to the people in the temple the whole message of this Life (Acts 5:20).

Notes

Notes

CHAPTER FOUR

RECRUIT. TRAIN. DEPLOY.

Now that we know what the mission of an Apostolic Assault Team is, we must discuss how to recruit soldiers. We should never rely solely on the tenured and seasoned soldiers. Just as the natural body has parts that continually develop new elements and regenerates within itself, the body of Christ is a living entity that should continually grow and expand.

We will also discuss how to train and develop the soldiers that have been recruited so that they are effective and devastating once mobilized. Once they have been recruited, trained, and developed, we will discuss how to strategically implement and deploy them as part of the Apostolic Assault Team that is a powerful force, which can and will have a massive devastating effect on the kingdom of darkness.

HOW TO RECRUIT APOSTOLIC ASSAULT TEAM MEMBERS

Jesus said, "I will build my church." The Chief Apostle is Jesus Christ. In John 6:44 Jesus says, "No one can come to Me unless the Father who sent Me draws him." Therefore, God Himself is the recruiter of members for His church. But He tells us to go out (assault) into the highways and hedges and compel them to come to Him. Notice there are no four walls of a church building on the highways and hedges.

The strategy to recruit Apostolic Assault Team members is simple and clear. Because God does the work to draw all people to Him, our charge is to reveal to the kingdom of darkness who Jesus is. We do this by testifying of His love, mercy, grace, and power. The way we testify is dependent on the region and the needs in that area. We also expose light in the darkness. Just as John the Baptist came as a witness to bear witness of the Light that all might believe. When we bear witness of who Christ is to the lost, the Father does the work to draw all men to Jesus.

This is where the evangelists and the gifts of helps and mercy, among others, are critical to the execution of the strategy. The team members who operate in the office of evangelist have the capacity and the grace to target the lost and oppressed by sharing the testimony of Jesus Christ. The manner in which we testify varies, but many times, people will only be open to receive us when their needs are met. Jesus fed the 5,000 after they spent the day watching Him perform signs and miracles. John 6:26 says, Jesus answered them and said, "Most assuredly, I say to you, you seek Me, not because you saw the signs, but because you ate of the loaves and were filled."

This highlights the fact that it is only when we meet the natural needs of people that they will seek the answer to their spiritual needs. Jesus fed the multitude bread to fill their natural needs and as the Bread of Life, He met their spiritual needs.

Another strategy to testify of Jesus is to minister healing and deliverance in the kingdom of darkness. After the men who were possessed with demons were delivered in Matthew 8:28-33, they "went away into the city and told everything" (they testified). Before they could recognize the power and authority of Jesus, He first had to minister deliverance to them.

Training Your Team

Once the Lord sends you recruits, it is imperative that you train them so they understand their gifts and inheritance in the kingdom. Before you are able to train recruits and activate them in the team, it's imperative that they understand their authority and assignment. It's also necessary that the recruits abandon their old mindsets and attitudes to conform more fully to the Commander in Chief to be effective in the mission at hand.

How to Facilitate a Change of Mindset and Attitude

We begin the process of changing the mindset and attitude of the recruits by instilling the Word of God in their hearts and allowing Holy Spirit to reveal the errors in the way they have been living. Hebrews 4:1 tells us that the Word is sharper than a two-edged sword, piercing even to the division of soul and spirit. Cleaning and transforming a person after he or she has accepted salvation through Christ begins with renewing the mind. Romans 12:2 tells us not to be conformed to this world but be transformed by the renewing of your mind that you may prove what is that good, acceptable, and perfect will of God. The Word of God renews our minds and cleans us from the inside out.

Clean hands are important to have when we minister to the recruits as we lead them and they are cleansed by the Word.

Hidden in the hands of Moses and Aaron, You led your people like a flock of sheep (Psalm 77:20, MSG).

Who may ascend onto the mountain of the Lord? And who may stand in His holy place? He who has clean hands and a pure heart, Who has not lifted up his soul to what is false, Nor has sworn [oaths] deceitfully. He shall receive a blessing from the Lord, and righteousness from the God of his salvation (Psalm 24:3-5, AMP).

We must be sure that we are walking in integrity and the love of Christ as we work to clean up the recruits and strip them of their former beliefs. We want nothing to hinder their progress in the transformation process. At times, we will have to go up the mountain ahead of the recruits and lead them through the process. To facilitate that journey, it is important that our hands are clean, and our hearts are pure. This form of discipleship is a valuable strategy to lead the recruit through the process.

The cleaning and deliverance process can be messy.

Now the practices of the sinful nature are *clearly* evident: they are sexual immorality (total irresponsibility, lack of self-control), idolatry, sorcery, hostility, strife, jealousy, fits of anger, disputes, dissensions, factions [that promote heresies], envy, drunkenness, riotous behavior, and other things like these. I warn you beforehand, just as I did previously, that those who practice such things will not inherit the kingdom of God (Galatians 5:19-21, AMP).

Because the deliverance process can be messy, we must be able to handle the mess without judgment or criticism. Instead, we should do so by expressing compassion and love. Offering the recruit the grace to be messy through the transformation process instead of expecting instant perfection can go a long way to encouraging the recruit to endure the process. Deliverance is a process and many times, not an instant occurrence, "And so it was, that as they [the 10 lepers] went, they were cleansed" (Luke 17:14b).

How Do We Preserve the New Mindset?

The recruit is sanctified through God. "And the very God of peace sanctify you wholly; and I pray God your whole spirit and soul and body be preserved blameless unto the coming of our Lord Jesus Christ" (1 Thessalonians 5:23). God, Himself sets us apart and preserves us.

How Do We Teach Our Transformed and Preserved Recruits to Recruit Other Members?

We do so by yoking up with them, having them tag along with us as we demonstrate the way, and then joining us in doing what they see us do. Discipleship must be implemented with the recruits. The blueprint for discipleship was shown to us by Jesus Christ. As He drew people to the Father, He allowed them to walk with Him to see how He handled every trial, temptation, opposition, and assault against the kingdom of darkness. As growth and maturity occur, we then step back and allow Holy Spirit to work through them. All the while, we provide accountability, encouragement, and instruction.

During the transformation process and then through discipleship, the team members are to be taught about the individual spiritual gifts they carry. A spiritual gifts resource that will prove itself highly effective in your team's spiritual gifts discovery can be found at mintools.com. These resources can be used at zero cost to you and your team members. It is important that the recruits are trained in how spiritual gifts are to be employed corporately, including order and protocol. Spiritual gifts that flow in the Spirit of God's love are vital in retaining the recruits that are enlisted. Frankly speaking, spiritual gifts that are effectively employed will nullify the swinging-door-effect that we see daily in so many local churches globally.

It is essential that the new team members know the fundamentals of the faith, including Christology, how to pray, how to effectively fulfill/demonstrate the new commandment of the New Testament church, which is to love and edify one another, and how to employ their spiritual gifts effectively as one single weapon of war in the hands of God.

In addition to the most important resource, the Holy Bible, some of the best additional training resources are listed below:

Prayers That Rout Demons by Apostle John Eckhardt
Moving in the Apostolic by Apostle John Eckhardt
School of the Apostles by Apostle Melvin Thompson III
School of the Prophets by Apostle Melvin Thompson III
Speak to the Mountains by Apostle Axel Sippach
Your Spiritual Gifts Can Help Your Church Grow by C. Peter Wagner

The only way to destroy the kingdom of darkness' assault is with Apostolic Assault.

Christ Jesus assaulted and destroyed the kingdom of darkness' assault in heaven.

Christ Jesus assaulted and destroyed the kingdom of darkness' assault on the earth.

Christ Jesus assaulted and destroyed the kingdom of darkness' assault in hell.

From the beginning of mankind, we were commanded to have dominion over the earth. Because we have been given the Spirit of Christ and the authority of Christ, we must confront and eradicate the kingdom of darkness in all areas that our feet tread upon.

Notes

Notes

CHAPTER FIVE

BUILDING UNDER GOD'S COMMANDS

Because we are created in God's image and likeness, we are creative people. In the kingdom, one mark of an apostle is the ability to build. We all have the apostolic character of a builder because we are made in His image. Scripture is filled with accounts of God giving His people instructions to build cities, towers, altars, temples, kingdoms, arks, tombs, and houses. We know that anything that is built on a firm foundation will stand. That sure foundation is Jesus (1 Corinthians 3:11). Therefore, as we begin to build an Apostolic Assault Team, it is important to know that the blueprint of what we are building is from God.

One sure way of testing whether or not God tells you to build something is what I call The Noah Test. Let's ask Noah regarding this. In Genesis 6-9, we can clearly see how this applies to you and me as well.

Just as God downloaded an apostolic mindset into the mind of Noah and told him what to build, the Lord Himself will download an apostolic mindset (kingdom mindset) into you as well. Then He will tell you:

- What to build
- How to build it
- Where to build it
- Who to build it with
- Who should remain a part of what is to be built

Then He will put the aroma of His glory upon you to draw the people and the resources you need to join Him in building His church. **God the Holy Spirit is the Builder**

Various Schemes of Maneuver in Conducting the Apostolic Assault and Take the Ekklesia from the Synagogue to Society

The ultimate objective of apostolic assault is the reconciliation of humanity to God.

> For it pleased the Father that in Him all the fullness should dwell, and by Him to reconcile all things to Himself, by Him, whether things on earth or things in heaven, having made peace through the blood of His cross (Colossians 1:19-20).

The most effective strategy for executing apostolic assault is operating in the likeness of Christ. Our focus must be to exemplify Christ in all that we do everywhere that we are. We must strive to be people of integrity and upright character so that all see Christ through us. It is not only important to *do* for people but also to *be* that salt and light. In addition, our individual and corporate focus must turn from self and our small circle to global. From the first day of training, a soldier is trained to be accountable for his brother.

"No man left behind." "If one fails, we all fail." We must take on that same mindset and compassion for our fellow man.

Tactics that should yield maximum impact in the marketplace are:

1. Demonstrated love in the form of giving
2. Free food on God
3. Free gifts to coworkers on God
4. Offering prayer for free to coworkers. Being a blessing to those in our sphere of influence is an effective tactic to draw others to Jesus

Tactics in the community are:

1. Assistance with utilities paid on God
2. Free community fair on God, free feeding the hungry on God
3. Free clothing to the naked on God
4. Free sheltering of the homeless on God

Apostle Melvin Thompson III has mastered these maneuvers with his team of believers in Harrisburg, PA at All Nations Evangelistic Church. When we have an assault strategy that has been effective in other regions, we can deploy the same strategy in another region, tailoring it to the specific needs of that region.

Tactics in local assemblies:

1. Conducting outdoor services
2. Being transparent and responsible by publishing accurate accountability

of funds collected by the ministries so that people will know what is being done with the tithes and offerings (integrity)

3. Visibly manifested signs and wonders

4. Feeding the multitudes outside in the community for all to see

Tactics in government:

1. Take the church to city halls and preach the gospel

2. Give gifts to city officials on God to show appreciation and encouragement

3. Give monies to the city government on God

4. Take back the dependency upon the government and replace it with dependence upon the Ekklesia.

Tactics in education:

1. Free business expos/entrepreneurial training of youth on God.

Tactics in the family:

1. Family prayer vigils at cookouts

2. Family confession vigils

Tactics in media:

Conduct a Super Bowl of Mass Deliverance addressing mass shootings in America. We need to have a Super Bowl of Mass Deliverance! While the world has its mind fixed on gun control, God has demon control on His mind because God knows that the only way to stop mass shootings in America is to have mass deliverance from demons inside the people in America. Let's have a "Super Bowl of Mass Deliverance from Demons" in America. Let it be broadcast live globally by every TV network in America just as it is done for the NFL.

#lettheworldseethepowerofGODgloballyatTheSuperBowl

#stadiumsallacrossthisnationwillsoonbefilledwithpeopleofallclassesseekingdeliverancefromdemonization

#letsmakeAmericaGodconsciousagain

#letsfilluptheSuperBowl

#everyoneisinvitedtoattend #signseekersneedtoseesigns

#GODneedstobeglorifiedglobally

#demonsneedtobecastout Facebook lives, Periscope, radio broadcasts

Reconnaissance Missions

Prior to employing an assault, it is necessary to deploy people into the region to determine the needs of the people in that area. This will help determine the most effective weapons in your arsenal and to prepare the way for the arrival of the Apostolic Assault Team. The 12 spies were deployed to scout the Promised Land and Joshua and Caleb returned with a revelation of the layout of the land and ultimate victory. That is the pattern for the Apostolic Assault Team of today. Answers to some questions such as:

- What is the economic condition of the area?

- What are the various demographics of the area, including ethnic diversity, median age, religious structure, and education level?
- What is the homeless rate?
- What is the condition of the local government?
- Are there common concerns with the health care system in the area?
- What are the needs of the education system?

It is vital to understand the history of the region, as well as the potential strongholds, principalities, and princes of the power of the air that may exist.

An example of the necessity to be armed with the correct weapons is a case such as Flint, Michigan. If an Apostolic Assault Team shows up with books and clothing when what the city really needs is clean water, it would only cause the people to reject them before they even open their mouths. Jesus always understood the condition of the people He ministered to. He had the insight and the compassion to recognize exactly where the people were at that moment. We must work to have that same understanding.

Armed with this intelligence, the Apostolic Assault Team will then be able to assess all of the resources, gifts, strengths, and weaknesses that exist in the troop to formulate a tactical plan. This plan may include partnering with another Apostolic Assault Team that specializes in an area of assault that is not developed in the local body of Christ.

Notes

Notes

CHAPTER SIX

SELFISH AMBITION AND THE SCHOOL OF DO NOTHING

Beware of Selfish Ambition

Team members must be free of selfish ambition. Selfish ambition is the root of pride!

Selfish ambition = devoted to or caring only for oneself; concerned primarily with one's own interests, benefits, welfare, etc., regardless of others; characterized by or manifesting concern or care only for oneself: selfish motives.

> Let nothing be done through selfish ambition or conceit, but in lowliness of mind let each esteem others better than himself (Philippians 2:3).

Just as the love of money is the root of all evil in the natural realm, selfish ambition is the root of all evil in the spiritual realm.

Pride is evil.

> For all that is in the world—the lust of the flesh, the lust of the eyes, and the pride of life—is not of the Father but is of the world (1 John 2:16).

48

Selfish ambition is the one elephant in the room that is hidden within the hearts of most of God's leaders. It creates all of the divisiveness we see in the body of Christ.

Selfish ambition causes us to seek recognition and promotion for ourselves, instead of the recognition and promotion of Jesus. If all the team members remain humble and keep the ultimate mission of assaulting the kingdom of darkness and glorifying Jesus in their sights, selfish ambition will have no place in our hearts.

> Some indeed preach Christ even from envy and strife, and some also from goodwill: [a]The former preach Christ from selfish ambition, not sincerely, supposing to add affliction to my chains; but the latter out of love, knowing that I am appointed for the defense of the gospel (Philippians 1:15-17).

Selfish ambition was found in the heart of God's anointed leader in heaven.

> I will ascend above the tops of the clouds; I will make myself like the Most High" - Lucifer (Isaiah 14:14).

Selfish ambition leads to discontentment, which, in turn, leads a person to become dissatisfied with who God created him or her to be. Consequently, that person dishonors God, which, in turn, leads to God-dishonoring the person who is contaminated with selfish ambition.

> Therefore, this is the declaration of the LORD, the God of Israel: 'Although I said your family and your ancestral house would walk before Me forever, the LORD now says, 'No longer!' I will honor those

who honor Me, but those who despise Me will be dis-graced (1 Samuel 2:30).

Selfish ambition causes one to refuse to submit to God, God's leadership, God's will, and/or submit to God's leaders.

THE SCHOOL OF DO NOTHING

The best way to work in harmony as a unified Apostolic Assault Team is to ensure that all team members attend and graduate from the School of Do Nothing.

> Do nothing out of selfish ambition or vain conceit. Rather, in humility value others above yourselves - THE WORD (Philippians 2:3).

The Lord demands that all members of His body come to His School of "DO NOTHING" immediately. In His school, you will learn how to Do Nothing out of selfish ambition or vain conceit.

Do No miracles . . . OUT OF SELFISH AMBITION OR VAIN CONCEIT

Do No signs . . . OUT OF SELFISH AMBITION OR VAIN CONCEIT

Do No wonders . . . OUT OF SELFISH AMBITION OR VAIN CONCEIT

Do No preaching . . . OUT OF SELFISH AMBITION OR VAIN CONCEIT

Do No teaching . . . OUT OF SELFISH AMBITION OR VAIN CONCEIT

Do No shepherding . . . OUT OF SELFISH AMBITION OR VAIN CONCEIT

Do No evangelizing . . . OUT OF SELFISH AMBITION OR VAIN CONCEIT

Do No apostleship . . . OUT OF SELFISH AMBITION OR VAIN CONCEIT

Do No praying . . . OUT OF SELFISH AMBITION OR VAIN CONCEIT

Do No spiritual leadership . . . OUT OF SELFISH AMBITION OR VAIN CONCEIT

Do No conferences . . . OUT OF SELFISH AMBITION OR VAIN CONCEIT

Do No worshipping . . . OUT OF SELFISH AMBITION OR VAIN CONCEIT

Do No praising . . . OUT OF SELFISH AMBITION OR VAIN CONCEIT

Do No making of disciples . . . OUT OF SELFISH AMBITION OR VAIN CONCEIT

Do No casting out devils . . . OUT OF SELFISH AMBITION OR VAIN CONCEIT

Do No Facebook-lives . . . OUT OF SELFISH AMBITION OR VAIN CONCEIT

Notes

Notes

CHAPTER SEVEN

APOSTOLIC ASSAULT TEAM MEMBERS MUST BE A COVENANTAL PEOPLE

Genesis 17:9-14

The sign of a covenantal relationship is: can you be corrected?

As a spiritual father/leader/mentor, God instructed Abraham to cut [correct] all who were under his leadership according to the scriptures below.

You will Honor my covenant, you and your descendants, generation after generation. - GOD

This is the covenant that you are to honor, the covenant that pulls in all your descendants: Circumcise every male. - GOD

Circumcise by cutting off the foreskin of the penis; it will be the sign of the covenant between us. - GOD

Every male baby will be circumcised [cut] when he is eight days old, generation after generation—this includes house-born slaves and slaves bought from outsiders who are not blood kin. - GOD

Make sure you circumcise [CUT] both your own children and anyone brought in from the outside. That way my covenant will be cut into your body, a permanent mark of my permanent covenant. - GOD

An uncircumcised [uncut] male, one who has not had the foreskin of his penis cut off, will be cut off from his people—he has broken my covenant. - GOD

If you can't be cut [corrected] by your spiritual father/mentor/coach, you cannot be in covenant with them or the people who God has given them oversight of.

Uncut [uncorrected] people must be cut off from covenantal people.

Spiritual sons and daughters whose hearts are right desire to be cut [corrected] by the spiritual leadership/mentor/coach that God provides them with.

> For whom the Lord loves He corrects, Just as a father the son in whom he delights (Proverbs 3:12).

The sign of a covenantal relationship with a spiritual father/mentor/coach is this: can they cut [correct] you in love without you getting offended, getting an attitude, getting in the flesh, getting angry, rebelling, leaving, etc.? The correct response is to humble yourself, receive correction, and make the necessary adjustment. When you are in a covenantal relationship, you should always trust that the other person's desire is to see you grow and mature for the glory of God. Therefore, you understand that the discipline is for your growth and benefit.

God is the God of covenant, and God's people are people of covenant.

Covenantal people are honorable people who gladly receive discipline from their spiritual leadership; hence, they are never homeless, roaming from spiritual leader to spiritual leader to spiritual leader after they are cut [corrected].

Covenantal people embrace correction [cutting] and then they live honored lives (Hebrews 12:9, CEV). Our earthly fathers correct us, and we still respect them. Isn't it even better to be given true life by letting our spiritual Father correct us?

Our cry as sons and daughters of God and of the spiritual leadership He has entrusted to us should be, "Father, lovingly cut me [correct me], please, and cut me deep with Your Word of correction so that I will mature into the fullness of the image and likeness of You. I embrace Your correction [cutting], so I can live an honored life."

Notes

Notes

CHAPTER EIGHT

CONCLUSION

What is God Doing in the Earth Now?

God is reforming His church to its original form—without selfish ambition. It is the church that has neither spot nor wrinkle. It is the church prior to when selfish ambition was found in the heart of Lucifer in heaven, and the church found in the book of Acts where selfish ambition could not dwell.

To reform something means to bring it back to its original form or to remove imperfections from a perfect thing. God is returning for His bride [His body, His Ekklesia, His Apostolic Assault Team] without spot or wrinkle.

Oh, how I pray that you would lay aside all selfish ambition and vain conceit to work together in honor, love, and submission to Christ and the members of His body as a unified team. Amen. For we are one body with the same Spirit. Just like a military assault team, the goal and mission must be the same for every member to work as a unit.

The day of the synagogue-syndrome and lone-ranger Christianity is over. But if you want to use God to make a name for yourself or to make yourself look important, go into ministry alone. A common tactic to destroy someone is to separate him from the group or divide and conquer. You become an easy target for the kingdom of darkness when you believe that you can be more successful on your own. But, if you want to fulfill the Master's dream/commission, go into the world as an Apostolic Assault Team.

I'm taken aback when I think about how easily we will conquer this world overnight for Christ Jesus when we crucify selfish ambition, honor one another, and work together as a team.

As we conduct apostolic assaults, please be mindful and know that there is no race, creed, or color in the kingdom of God.

> For as many of you as were baptized into Christ have put on Christ. There is neither Jew nor Greek, there is neither slave nor free, there is neither male nor female; for you are all one in Christ Jesus. And if you are Christ's, then you are Abraham's seed, and heirs according to the promise (Galatians 3:27-29).

I prophesy to you that the spiritual campaign and apostolic assault that you are about to embark on will have tremendous God-success. You will conquer and recover all the dark territories in your region in the authority of Jesus Christ. Amen.

Notes

Notes